Shannon Moyer is a mental-health counsellor from London, Ontario. She processes emotion and inner thoughts through art and writing, leading her clients to do the same so as to understand themselves on a deeper level. Shannon is a believer in fundamental rights, standing up for oneself and being a kind and compassionate human being, leaving a positive impact wherever possible. When not writing or nurturing others, you can find her at the ski hill, horse barn or baseball diamond with her boys, or cuddled on the couch with her rescue dog, Berney.

In My Head

The ADHD Journal for Adults

by: Shannon Moyer

AUSTIN MACAULEY PUBLISHERS®

LONDON * CAMBRIDGE * NEW YORK * SHARJAH

Ordering Information

Quantity sales: Special discounts are available on quantity purchases by corporations, associations, and others. For details, contact the publisher at the address below.

Publisher's Cataloging-in-Publication data

Moyer, Shannon

In My Head

ISBN 9798889109433 (Paperback)

Library of Congress Control Number: 2024914843

www.austinmacauley.com/us

First Published 2024

Austin Macauley Publishers LLC

40 Wall Street, 33rd Floor, Suite 3302

New York, NY 10005

USA

mail-usa@austinmacauley.com

+1 (646) 5125767

For all of the adults coming to a new understanding of how their brains work within the realm of ADHD, this is for you.

When I was diagnosed with ADHD and ODD, I knew that I had intuitively been using tools rooted in writing and art for years as a way to allow my brain space to breathe and process the world around it. Seeing an incredible lack of resources for adults newly diagnosed with ADHD, I wanted to pull together these tools that I know work so well into a journal that could help others.

In My Head – The ADHD Journal for Adults was born, with so many more ideas for emotional regulation, processing, art exploration and writing milling around in the background.

To Graeme – thank you for showing up in the way that you do. We have learned so much from you by witnessing the world through your eyes of neurodiversity and without you, I would never have explored my own brain. This body of work was inspired by you and your beautiful brain. I love you.

To Owen – thank you for reminding me to slow down, take a breath, stop interrupting and jumping from topic to topic, and being a pure heart that this world needs. Turns out, your brain is like mine and we get to go on this journey together. I love you, Joe.

To Jeannette – thank you for challenging my concept of self and perspective. Thank you for pushing me to do and be better, so that I can be present for others. I love you, and when are we going to Heemans?

To Tanya, Michelle, Cass and Cassandra – your constant support, voice notes, hugs, concert dates, and checkins mean so much. You are some of the most true and incredible humans on the planet and I appreciate you.

To Carlen – thank you for creating spaces wherein ADHD is normalized and embraced. Thank you for continuing to show up, in a spaceship in the backyard, and for believing in me, personally and professionally.

To Sara – thank you for always being a shoulder to lean on, offering a word of reassurance, and for believing in me and my lived experience. I am so thankful that you are in my corner.

To all of the weirdos, misfits, black sheep, troublemakers, loud ones and daydreamers – I see you. I am you. The world wasn't made for brains like ours, but we can change that by showing up as our true selves. We've got this. And you're important.

'Before you begin, I just want you to know.
Your thoughts are valid.
Your feelings are valid.
You are not broken.
Your brain just works differently, and that's
okay.'

—Shannon Moyer

Welcome to *In My Head – The ADHD Journal for Adults*! I was diagnosed with Inattentive ADHD at 40 years old. FORTY. We also sprinkled some ODD in there, because why not?

Immediately following my diagnosis, I started looking for resources, and knowing that I am a writer and artist at heart, I wanted the resources to have depth and meaning. What I found in my search were digital planners designed for organization, but I felt like I needed something tangible in my hands. I also found infographics and worksheets geared towards kids and their experience, but not a whole lot for adults.

Off to my toolkit I went, and I started considering how the tools I use in the counseling space could apply to people with ADHD. Then I started experimenting with them, and lo and behold…I started processing my ADHD experience differently.

I felt grounded and validated, and 'In My Head – the ADHD Journal for Adults' was born!

I hope the pages contained in this workbook-style journal give you space to find yourself and start working with your brain instead of pushing it into spaces that it simply wasn't designed for.

'There's nothing wrong with you. You just have ADHD.'
—Shannon Moyer

The How and Why

Using this journal is super easy, and it's all organized into three sections to help your brain stay on task. Unlike other journals and planners, there are prompts along the way designed specifically for ADHD brains so as to alleviate overwhelm, overstimulation, and give space for you to feel validated in your experience as a neurodiverse human!

Journal Prompts

These pages are designed to help you write out your thoughts and feelings in a way that validates your experience with ADHD. In this section, you will find tools for intrusive thoughts, rapid thought cycles, forgetfulness, validation, and balancing. There is also space for free journalling on lined pages.

Art Prompts

The Art Prompts section of this journal is the space where you get to give a physical representation of your ADHD. Using color, line, shape, and form (some of my favorite elements and principles of art and design) is such a great way to make sense of the ADHD experience when words don't quite fit. There are also blank pages at the end of this section, so let your creativity out!

Emotional Processing

The final section is all about emotional processing, so think of these pages like what you would get in the counseling space as homework assignments. They're the pages where you'll make connections, deal with intrusive thoughts, and allow yourself to decompress.

List of Things

List of Things

List of Things

List of Things

List of Things

List of Things

List of Things

-
-
-
-
-
-
-
-
-
-
-
-
-
-
-
-
-
-
-
-
-
-
-
-

List of Things

List of Things

List of Things

List of Things

-
-
-
-
-
-
-
-
-
-
-
-
-
-
-
-
-
-
-
-
-
-
-
-

List of Things

-
-
-
-
-
-
-
-
-
-
-
-
-
-
-
-
-
-
-
-
-
-
-

List of Things

List of Things

-
-
-
-
-
-
-
-
-
-
-
-
-
-
-
-
-
-
-
-
-
-

Symptom Tracker

Month: Year:

Observations:

Symptom Tracker

Month: Year:

Observations:

Symptom Tracker

Month: Year:

Observations:

Symptom Tracker

Month: Year:

Observations:

Symptom Tracker

Month: Year:

Observations:

Symptom Tracker

Month: Year:

Observations:

Symptom Tracker

Month: Year:

Observations:

Symptom Tracker

Month: Year:

Observations:

Symptom Tracker

Month: Year:

Observations:

Symptom Tracker

Month: Year:

Observations:

Symptom Tracker

Month: Year:

Observations:

Symptom Tracker

Month: Year:

Observations:

Journal Prompts

What Emotions am I currently feeling?

Why am I feeling this way?

What Emotions am I currently feeling?

Why am I feeling this way?

What Emotions am I currently feeling?

Why am I feeling this way?

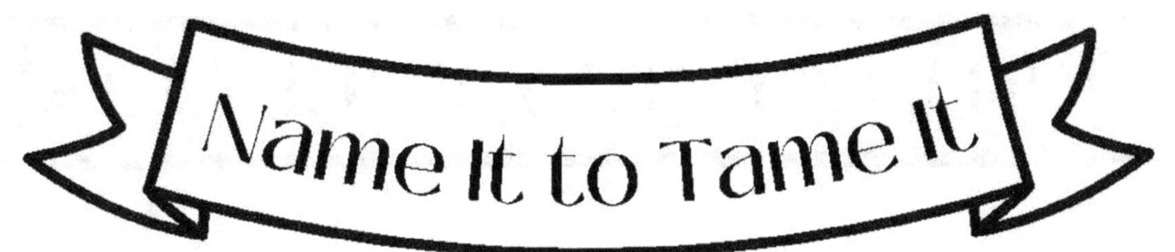

What Emotions am I currently feeling?

Why am I feeling this way?

Don't Forget About Me

Date:

Reminder:

Why do I need to remember this?

Don't Forget About Me

Date:

Reminder:

Why do I need to remember this?

Don't Forget About Me

Date:

Reminder:

Why do I need to remember this?

Don't Forget About Me

Date:

Reminder:

Why do I need to remember this?

Date:

Reminder:

Why do I need to remember this?

Thought Spirals

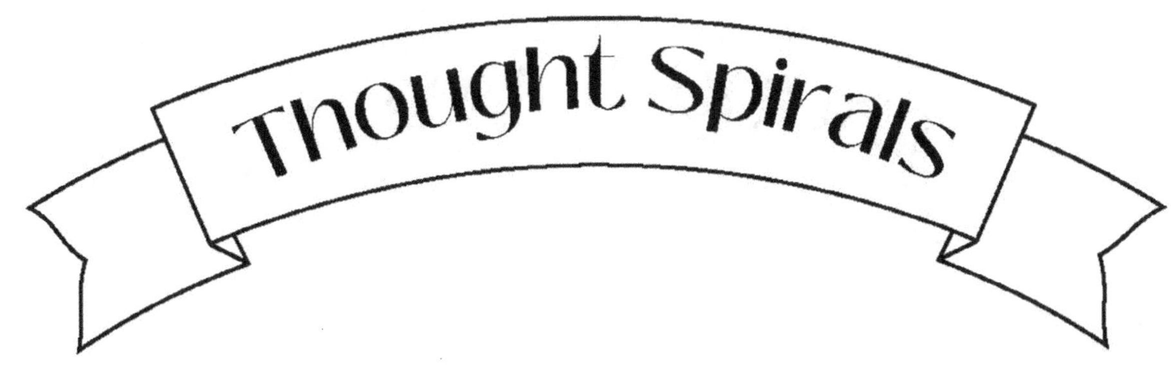

Anxious, intrusive thoughts can pull you into a spiral. Instead of getting sucked into the vortex, write it out.

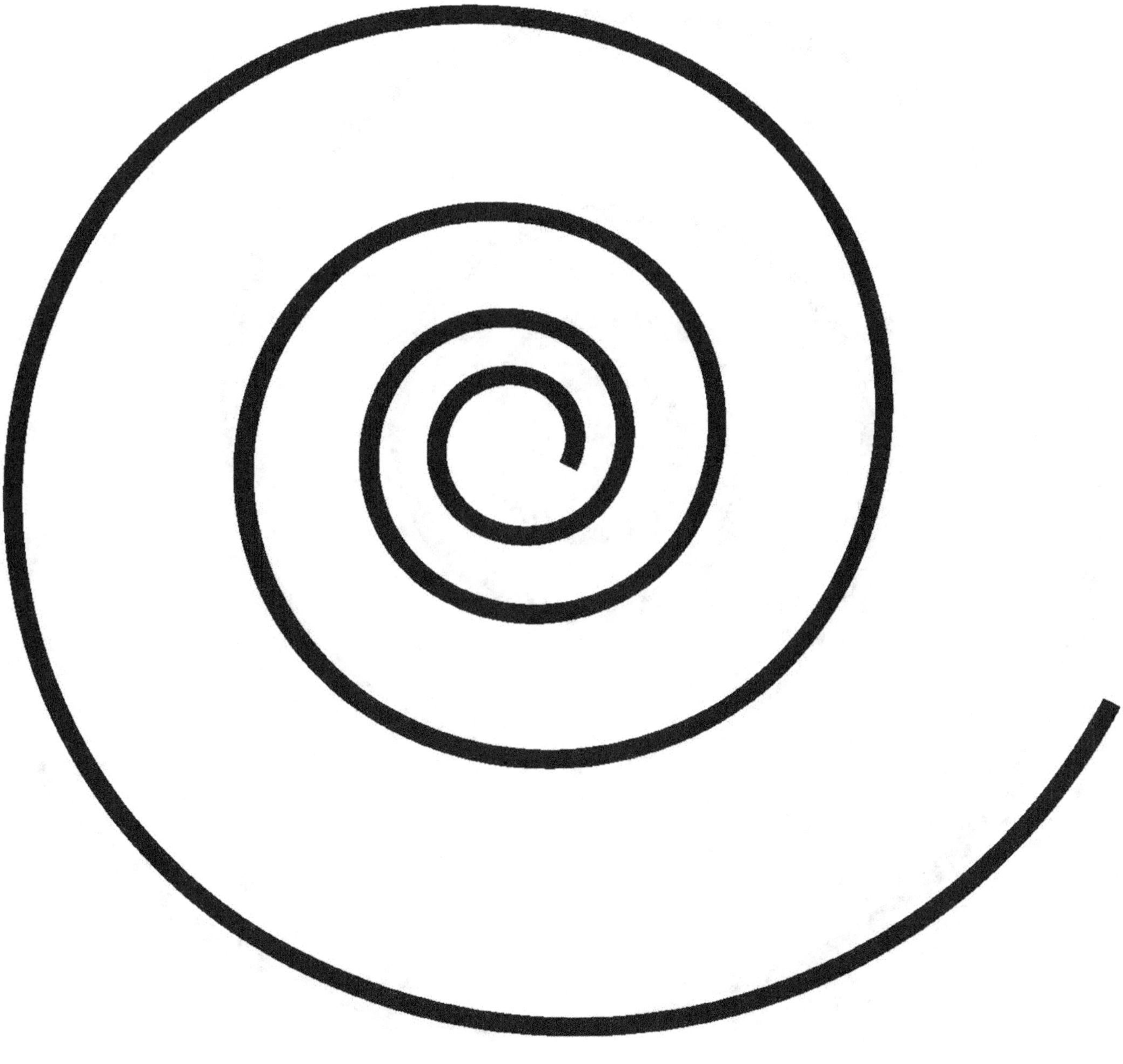

How do you feel after?

Thought Spirals

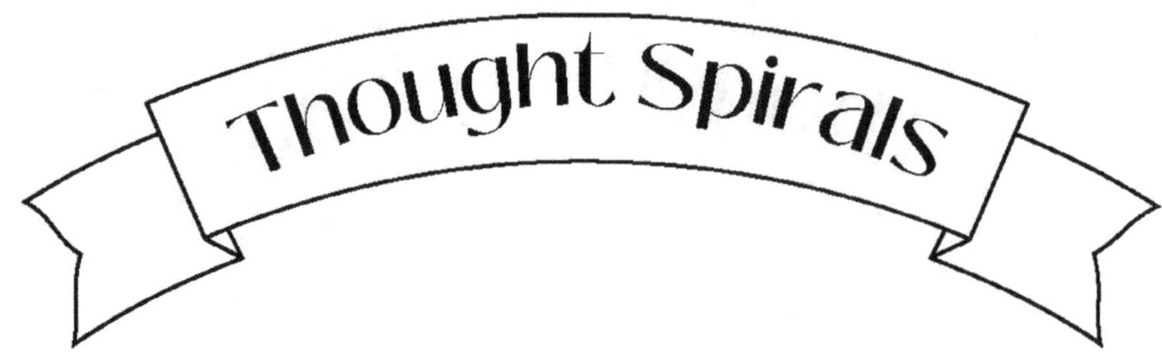

Anxious, intrusive thoughts can pull you into a spiral.
Instead of getting sucked into the vortex, write it out.

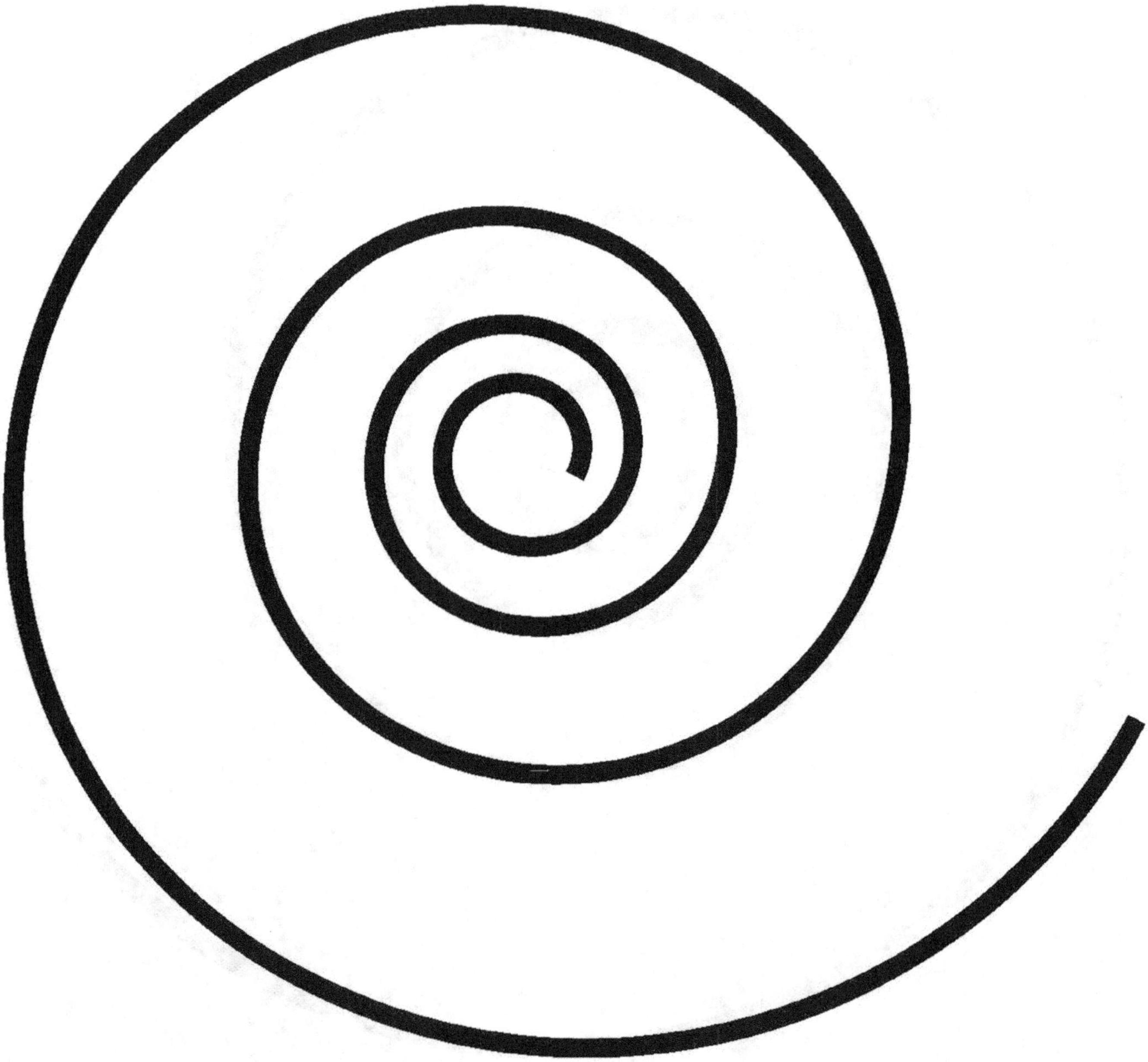

How do you feel after?

Thought Spirals

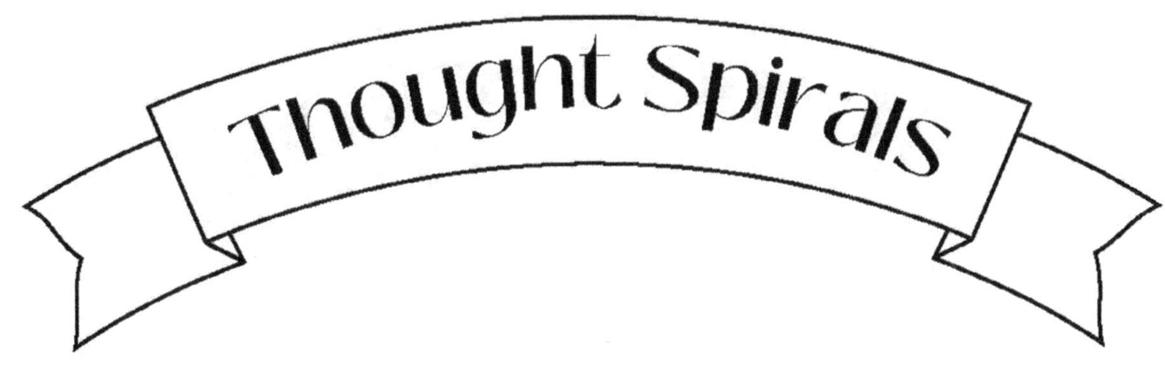

Anxious, intrusive thoughts can pull you into a spiral.
Instead of getting sucked into the vortex, write it out.

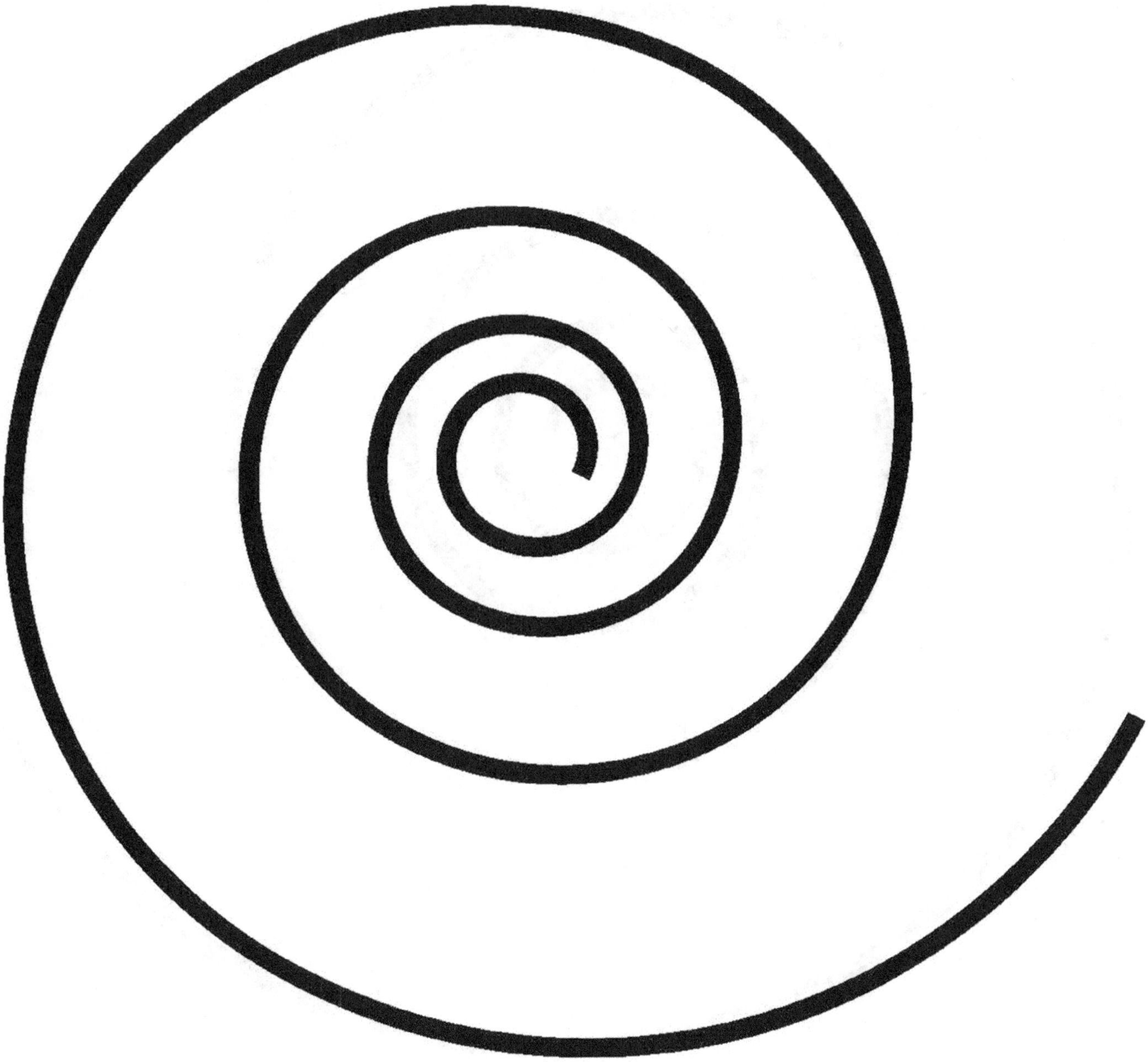

How do you feel after?

Thought Spirals

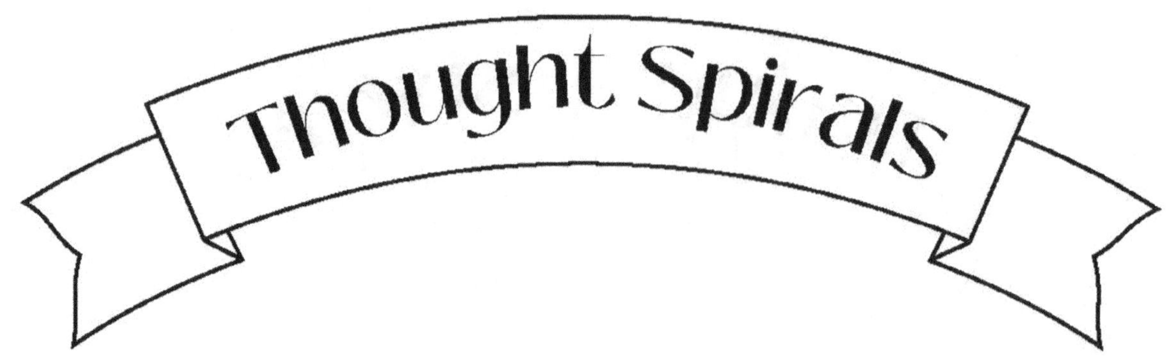

Anxious, intrusive thoughts can pull you into a spiral.
Instead of getting sucked into the vortex, write it out.

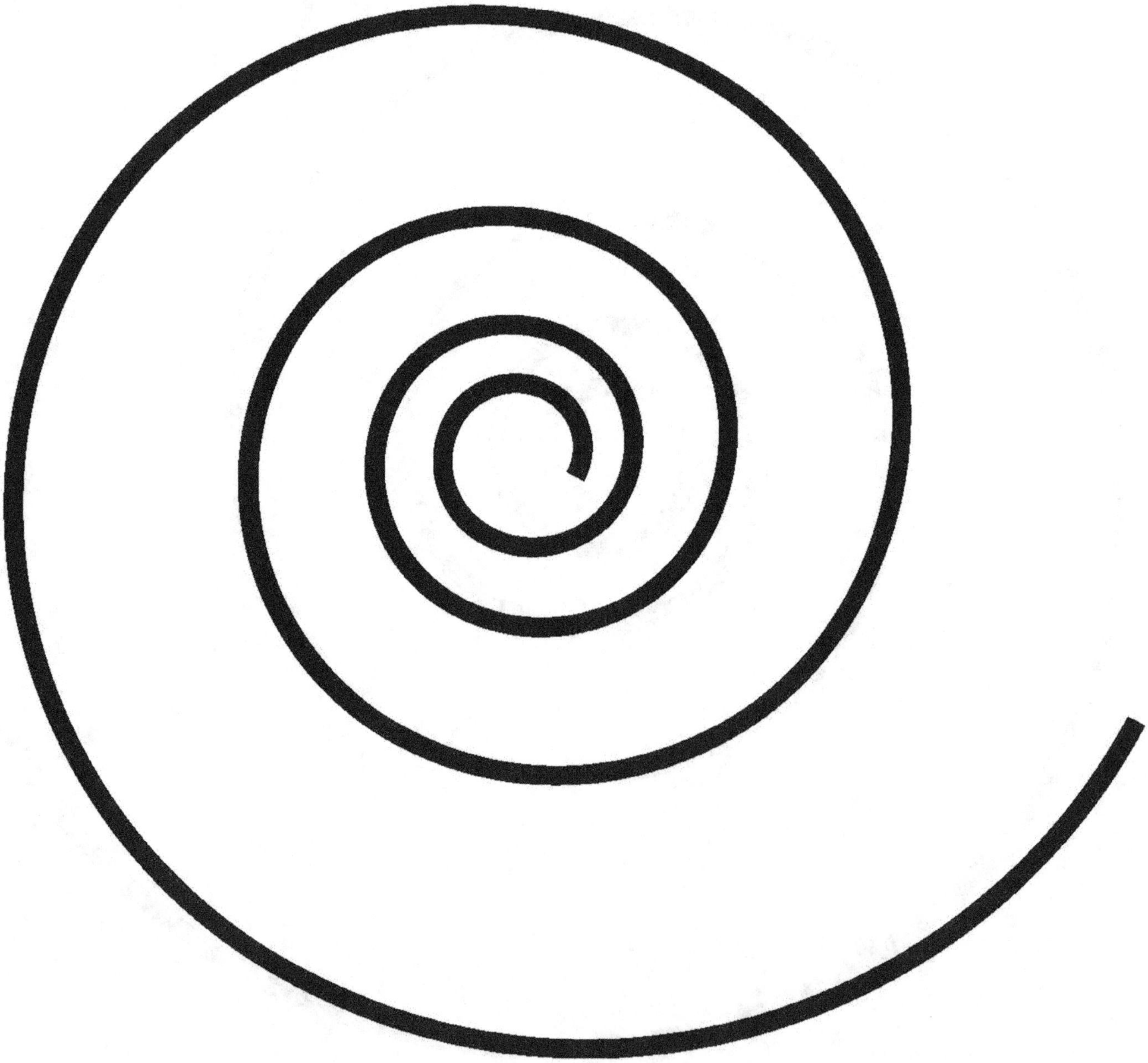

How do you feel after?

Thought Spirals

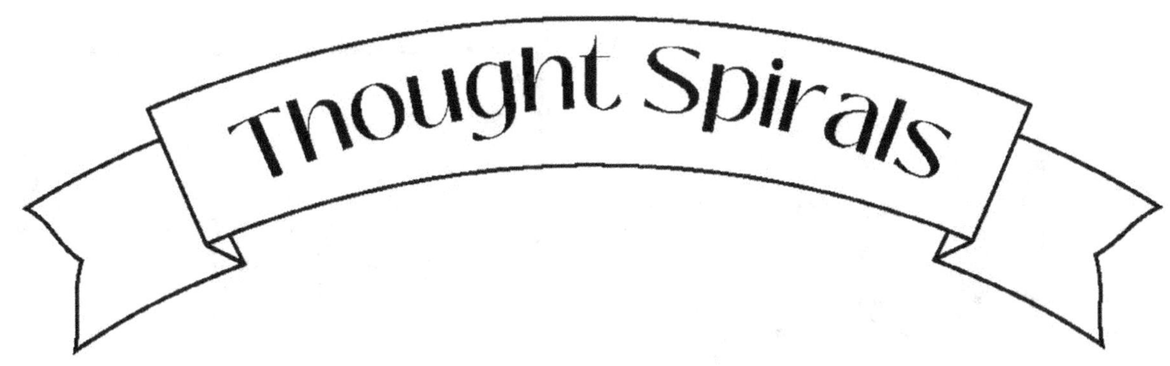

Anxious, intrusive thoughts can pull you into a spiral. Instead of getting sucked into the vortex, write it out.

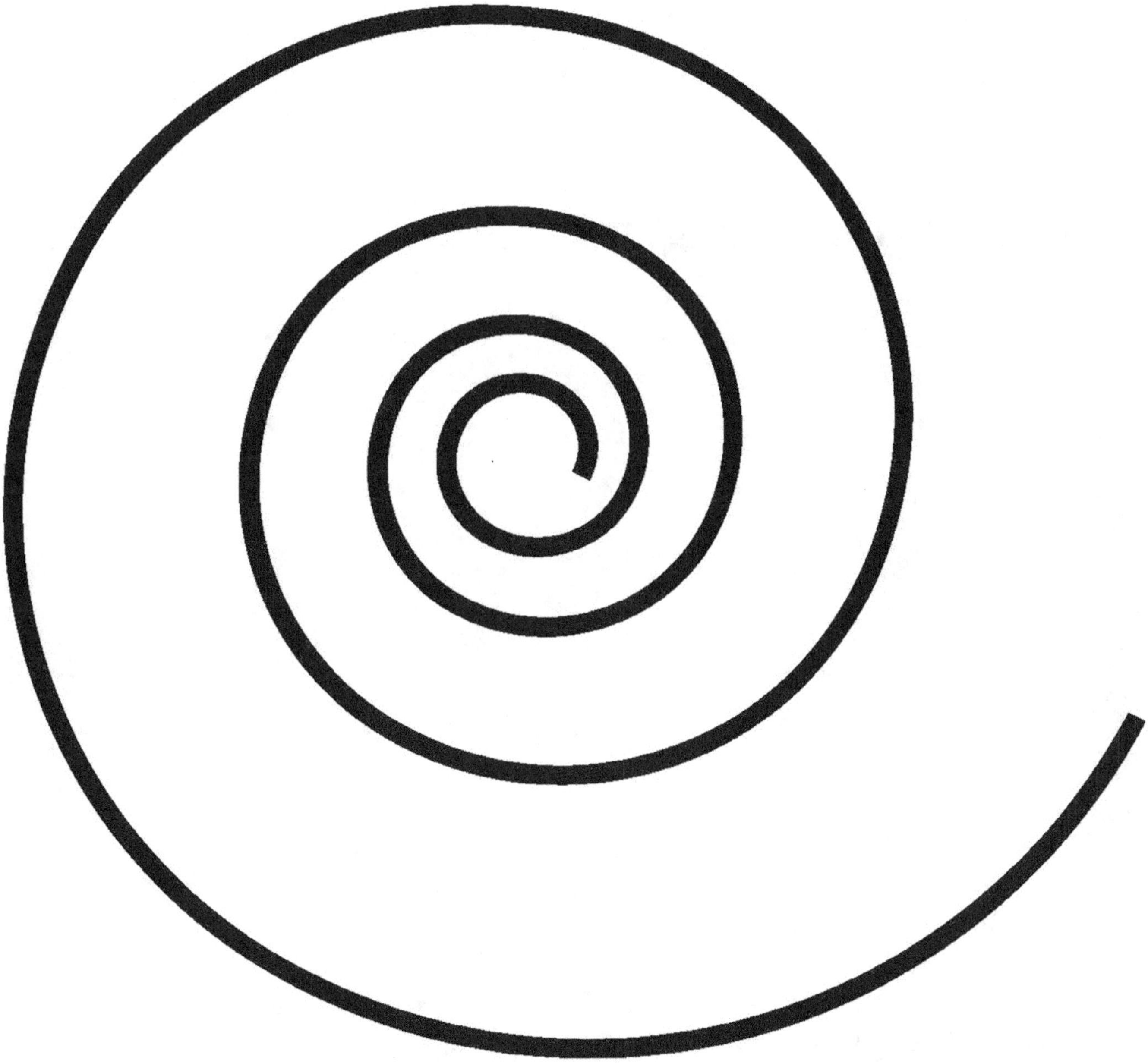

How do you feel after?

Joy 

Dopamine down and you feel like you are spiraling? Try a Joy Task!

These tasks bring me joy:

-
-
-
-
-
-
-
-
-
-

How do I feel after a joy task?

Joy 

Dopamine down and you feel like you are spiraling? Try a Joy Task!

These tasks bring me joy:

-
-
-
-
-
-
-
-
-
-

How do I feel after a joy task?

Joy Tasks

Dopamine down and you feel like you are spiraling? Try a Joy Task!

These tasks bring me joy:

-
-
-
-
-
-
-
-
-

How do I feel after a joy task?

Joy 

Dopamine down and you feel like you are spiraling? Try a Joy Task!

These tasks bring me joy:

-
-
-
-
-
-
-
-
-

How do I feel after a joy task?

Joy  Tasks

Dopamine down and you feel like you are spiraling? Try a Joy Task!

These tasks bring me joy:

-
-
-
-
-
-
-
-
-

How do I feel after a joy task?

Parking Lot

Your thoughts matter, each one is valid.

Parking Lot

Your thoughts matter, each one is valid.

Parking Lot

Your thoughts matter, each one is valid.

Date:

Date:

Date:

Date:

Date:

Date:

Date:

Date:

Date:

Date:

Date:

Date:

Date:

Date:

Date:

Date:

Date:

Date:

Date:

Date:

Art
Prompts

Make - a - Line

If your ADHD were a line, what would it look like?

What does your ADHD look like?

Make - a - Line

If your ADHD were a line, what would it look like?

What does your ADHD look like?

Make - a - Line

If your ADHD were a line, what would it look like?

What does your ADHD look like?

Make - a - Line

If your ADHD were a line, what would it look like?

What does your ADHD look like?

Make - a - Line

If your ADHD were a line, what would it look like?

What does your ADHD look like?

As ADHDers, we often mask so as to fit in with expectations and societal situations. What would it look like if you took off your mask today?

____

As ADHDers, we often mask so as to fit in with expectations and societal situations. What would it look like if you took off your mask today?

____

As ADHDers, we often mask so as to fit in with expectations and societal situations. What would it look like if you took off your mask today?

____

As ADHDers, we often mask so as to fit in with expectations and societal situations. What would it look like if you took off your mask today?

As ADHDers, we often mask so as to fit in with expectations and societal situations. What would it look like if you took off your mask today?

____

Dopamine Rush

Dopamine is a mood boosting chemical in the brain known to give ADHDers a sense of accomplishment and reward. We can feel the rush, and often chase it with things like exercise, food, thrill seeking behaviours – but what would it look like if we turned it into art?

Dopamine Rush

Dopamine is a mood boosting chemical in the brain known to give ADHDers a sense of accomplishment and reward.
We can feel the rush, and often chase it with things like exercise, food, thrill seeking behaviours - but what would it look like if we turned it into art?

Dopamine Rush

Dopamine is a mood boosting chemical in the brain known to give ADHDers a sense of accomplishment and reward. We can feel the rush, and often chase it with things like exercise, food, thrill seeking behaviours – but what would it look like if we turned it into art?

Dopamine Rush

Dopamine is a mood boosting chemical in the brain known to give ADHDers a sense of accomplishment and reward. We can feel the rush, and often chase it with things like exercise, food, thrill seeking behaviours – but what would it look like if we turned it into art?

Dopamine Rush

Dopamine is a mood boosting chemical in the brain known to give ADHDers a sense of accomplishment and reward. We can feel the rush, and often chase it with things like exercise, food, thrill seeking behaviours – but what would it look like if we turned it into art?

ADHD has two sides: hyperactive and inattentive. If you were to map these two sides of your brain out, what would they look like?

ADHD has two sides: hyperactive and inattentive. If you were to map these two sides of your brain out, what would they look like?

ADHD has two sides: hyperactive and inattentive. If you were to map these two sides of your brain out, what would they look like?

ADHD has two sides: hyperactive and inattentive. If you were to map these two sides of your brain out, what would they look like?

ADHD has two sides: hyperactive and inattentive. If you were to map these two sides of your brain out, what would they look like?

What Colour is Your ADHD?

Color can help give context to emotion, Use this page to represent your ADHD with the use of color, then reflect on how it changes from day to day.

Date:

Date:

Date:

Color can help give context to emotion, Use this page to represent your ADHD with the use of color, then reflect on how it changes from day to day.

Date:

Date:

Date:

Color can help give context to emotion, Use this page to represent your ADHD with the use of color, then reflect on how it changes from day to day.

Date:

Date:

Date:

Color can help give context to emotion, Use this page to represent your ADHD with the use of color, then reflect on how it changes from day to day.

Date:

Date:

Date:

What Colour is Your ADHD?

Color can help give context to emotion, Use this page to represent your ADHD with the use of color, then reflect on how it changes from day to day.

Date:

Date:

Date:

Emotional Processing

Use this page to make connections to the emotions that you're feeling. Name it in the center, then write down what is connected to it.

Emotional Mapping

Use this page to make connections to the emotions that you're feeling. Name it in the center, then write down what is connected to it.

Emotional Mapping

Use this page to make connections to the emotions that you're feeling. Name it in the center, then write down what is connected to it.

Use this page to make connections to the emotions that you're feeling. Name it in the center, then write down what is connected to it.

Emotional Mapping

Use this page to make connections to the emotions that you're feeling. Name it in the center, then write down what is connected to it.

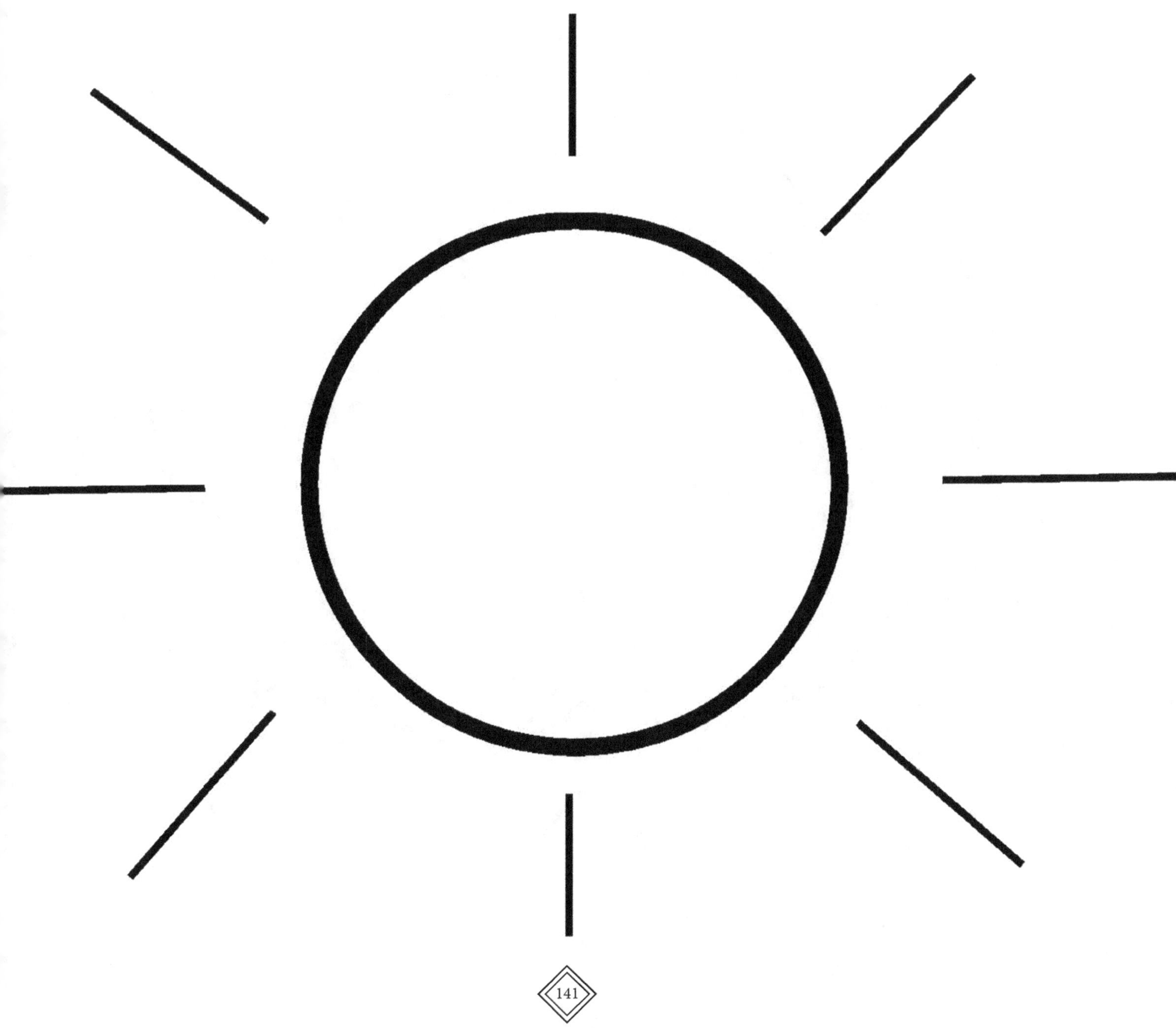

Thought | Monster

The darker side of ADHD is often intrusive and catastrophic thoughts. They feel real and can be scary, but what if we simply write them down or give them to a thought monster?

Thought Monster

The darker side of ADHD is often intrusive and catastrophic thoughts. They feel real and can be scary, but what if we simply write them down or give them to a thought monster?

Thought Monster

The darker side of ADHD is often intrusive and catastrophic thoughts. They feel real and can be scary, but what if we simply write them down or give them to a thought monster?

Thought Monster

The darker side of ADHD is often intrusive and catastrophic thoughts. They feel real and can be scary, but what if we simply write them down or give them to a thought monster?

Thought Monster

The darker side of ADHD is often intrusive and catastrophic thoughts. They feel real and can be scary, but what if we simply write them down or give them to a thought monster?

Rapid thought cycles are common for those with ADHD. Use the quadrants below to dump out and categorize your thoughts, with the intention of moving them forward.

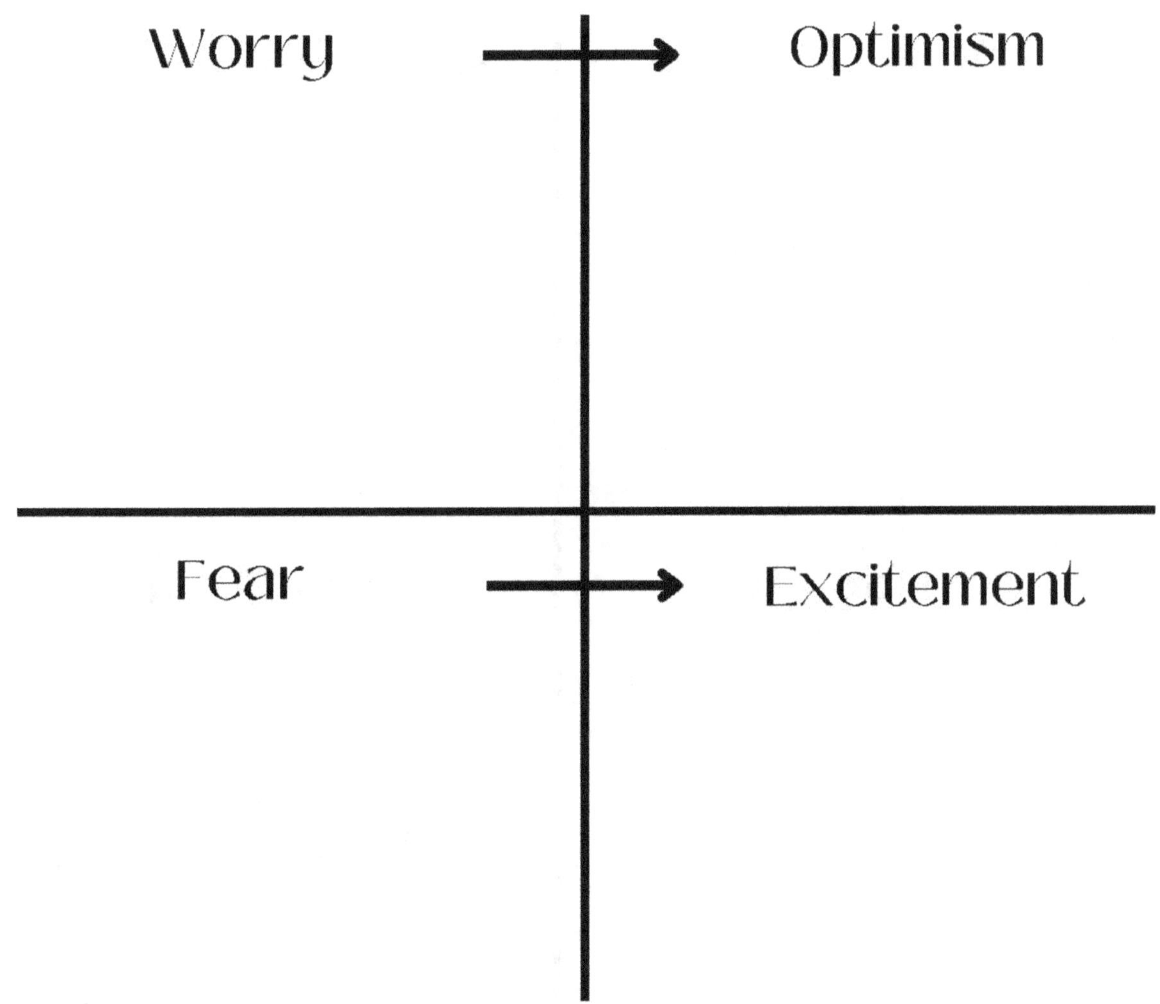

Move your thoughts forward out of the dark.

Rapid thought cycles are common for those with ADHD. Use the quadrants below to dump out and categorize your thoughts, with the intention of moving them forward.

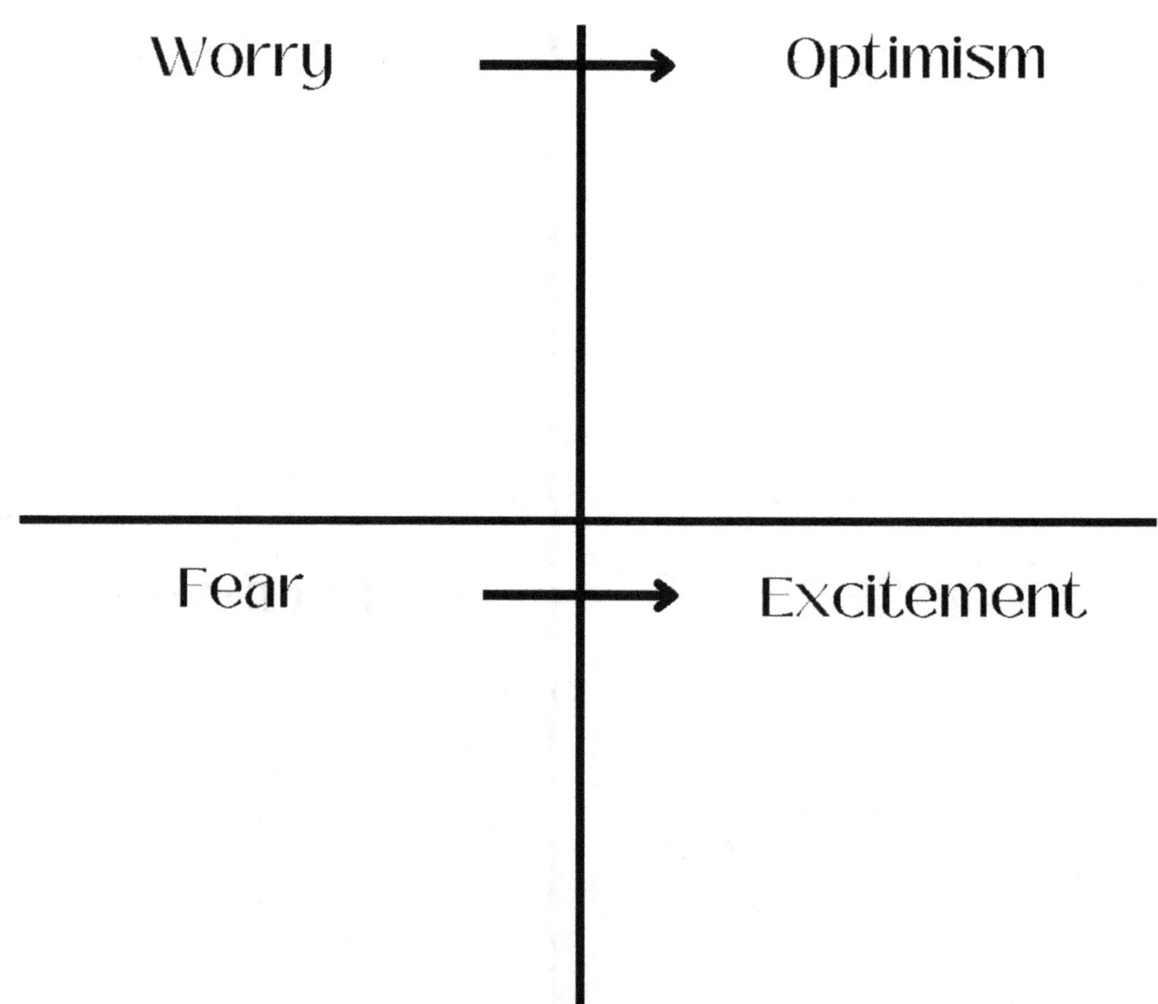

Move your thoughts forward out of the dark.

Rapid thought cycles are common for those with ADHD. Use the quadrants below to dump out and categorize your thoughts, with the intention of moving them forward.

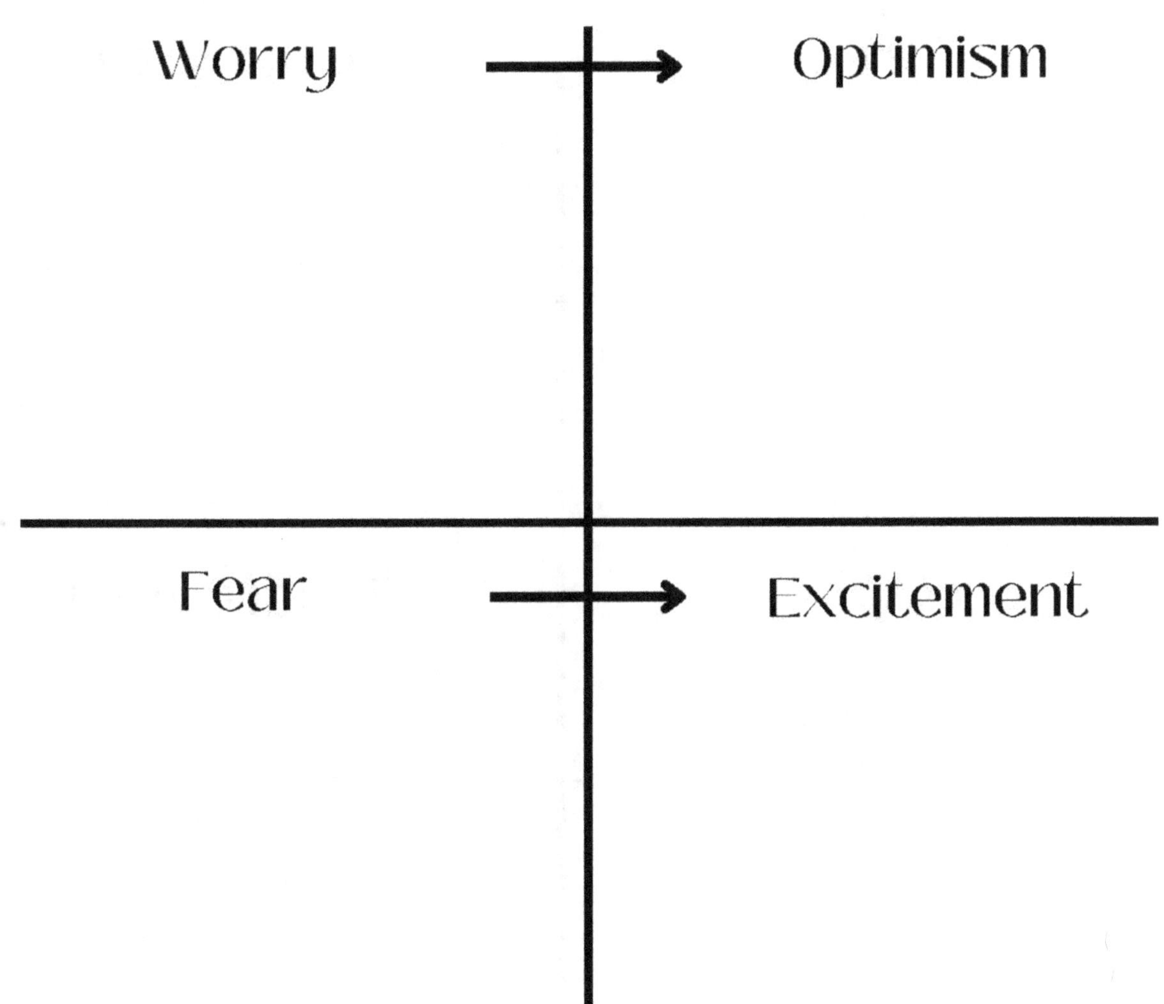

Move your thoughts forward out of the dark.

Rapid thought cycles are common for those with ADHD. Use the quadrants below to dump out and categorize your thoughts, with the intention of moving them forward.

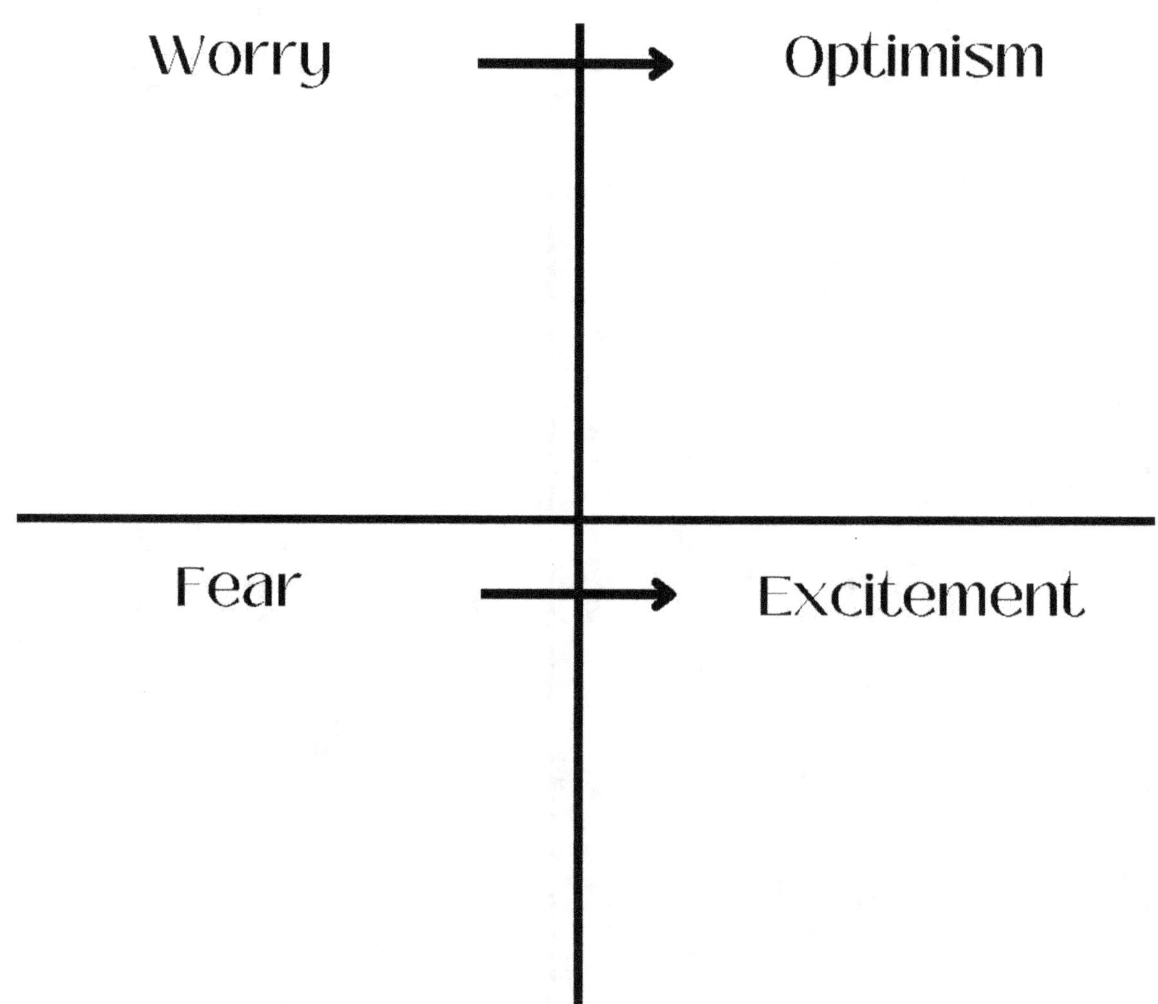

Move your thoughts forward out of the dark.

Rapid thought cycles are common for those with ADHD. Use the quadrants below to dump out and categorize your thoughts, with the intention of moving them forward.

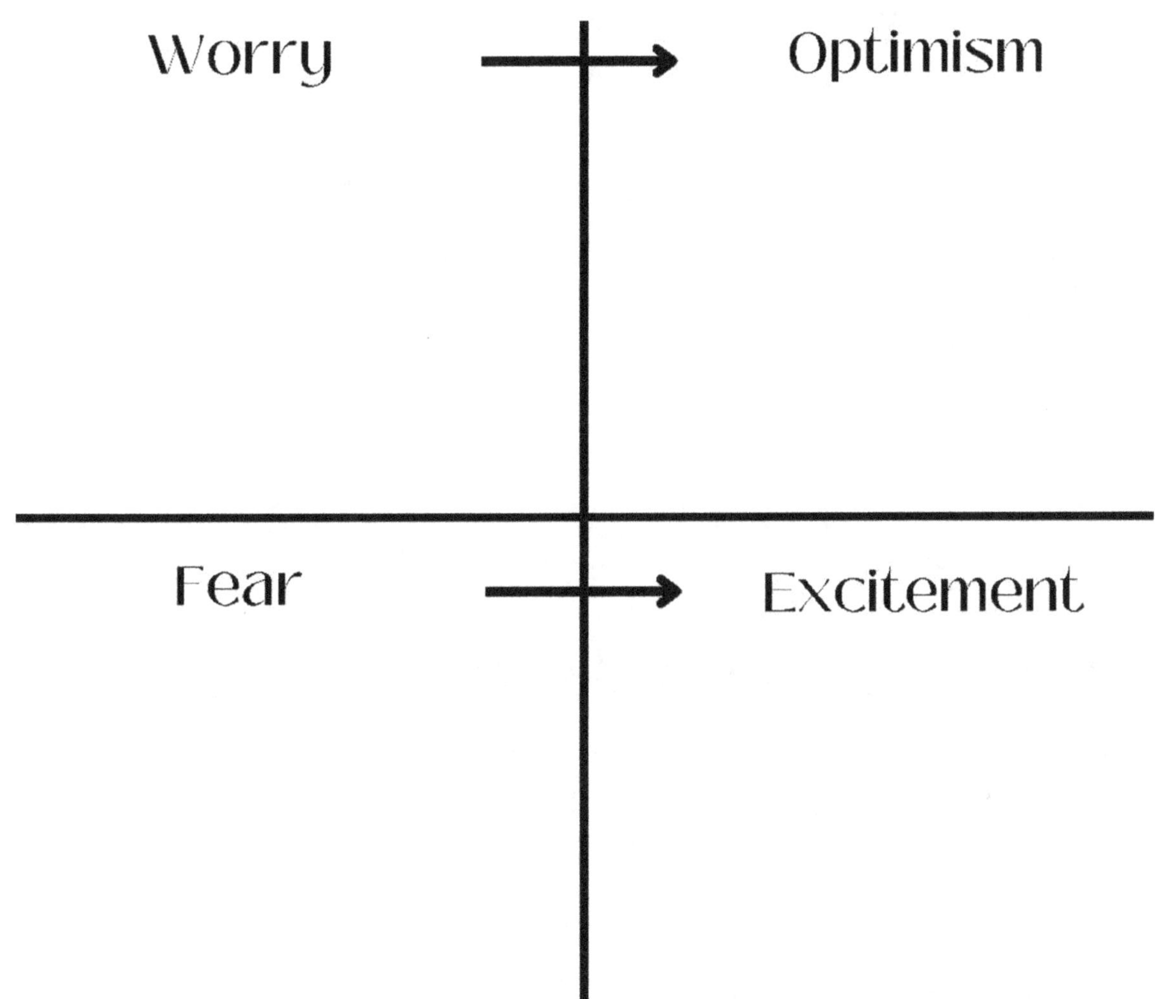

Move your thoughts forward out of the dark.

For a deeper dive into emotional reactions and outbursts, use this page as a space to reflect on your actions and consider your behavior as a form of communication.

Date:

What happened?

How I reacted?

What I was trying to communicate?

An Alternative Reaction:

Decompression Time

For a deeper dive into emotional reactions and outbursts, use this page as a space to reflect on your actions and consider your behavior as a form of communication.

Date:

What happened?

How I reacted?

What I was trying to communicate?

An Alternative Reaction:

For a deeper dive into emotional reactions and outbursts, use this page as a space to reflect on your actions and consider your behavior as a form of communication.

Date:

What happened?

How I reacted?

What I was trying to communicate?

An Alternative Reaction:

Decompression Time

For a deeper dive into emotional reactions and outbursts, use this page as a space to reflect on your actions and consider your behavior as a form of communication.

Date:

What happened?

How I reacted?

What I was trying to communicate?

An Alternative Reaction:

Decompression Time

For a deeper dive into emotional reactions and outbursts, use this page as a space to reflect on your actions and consider your behavior as a form of communication.

Date:

What happened?

How I reacted?

What I was trying to communicate?

An Alternative Reaction:

This may be the end of the journal, but it is not the end of your journey through ADHD. Use these tools as often as you need them and know that they are always here for you. Remember, you're not broken, You just have ADHD.